Wild Dialectics

Other works by Lisa Samuels include:

LETTERS (Meow Press 1996)
The Seven Voices (O Books 1998)
War Holdings (Pavement Saw Press 2003)
Paradise for Everyone (Shearsman Books 2005)
Increment (a family romance) (Bronze Skull Press 2006)
The Invention of Culture (Shearsman Books 2008)
Throe (Oystercatcher Press 2009)
Tomorrowland (Shearsman Books 2009)
Mama Mortality Corridos (Holloway Press 2010)
Gender City (Shearsman Books 2011)

LISA SAMUELS

Wild Dialectics

Shearsman Books

First published in the United Kingdom in 2012 by
Shearsman Books Ltd
50 Westons Hill Drive
Emersons Green
BRISTOL
BS16 7DF

Shearsman Books Ltd Registered Office
30–31 St. James Place, Mangotsfield, Bristol BS16 9JB
(this address not for correspondence)

www.shearsman.com

ISBN 978-1-84861-257-0

Cover art by Laura McLauchlan.

Acknowledgements
Versions of some of these poems have appeared in
Birkbeck Contemporary Poetics (Carol Watts),
Brief and *Percutio* (Bill Direen),
Hambone (Nathaniel Mackey), *Otoliths* (Mark Young),
Ping Pong (James Maughn), *Shadowtrain* (Ian Seed),
and *Spoon River Poetry Review* (Kirstin Hotelling Zona).
My thanks to the editors (named).

Contents

piling-up is the most suitable technique for exposing a reality that is itself being scattered

Édouard Glissant, *Caribbean Discourse*

Logic can't explain water, though wet elucidates thought. A kiss then
Moistens within, and speech glistens. That's talk's use: such internal
Circuitry. Where shapes drip into liquid's a formation, a source, planet
Or braid, tapering. Anyone's relation to invisibilities might be most sensed
In gravity, the shadows of dimensions, as weight propagates, as in only
Mass spreads multiple enough. But why should all shattering break down to
Some indivisible chord? Where duration boomerangs, sound can't tell,
Though the particles at stake may glow; perhaps infinitesimally felt.

Stacy Doris, *Knot*

Rise

The south is perforated by axiom, a kind of young acceleration

crab claws hanging out of a mouth, a cave mouth, the cave dwindled to
a salt pool mini-deep

illumining humans with micro-attitude, approach because especially

the seat on which the subject sits humane, of the many salt sidings we
could choose

this one has the visitation framed as narrow bands the voice

of the sidling firstness, little eyes opening their wax pragmatics with
ecstatic treason

fingering you sauvage straight through (your eyes) where you invigorate
were kindly

on the leas, where we undealt you on the made a part (of) when?

On the level

Wakeful

Break, came with an arms, the head gentle tiering
bookish, serene as automobiles through the wind

cam ready to fish, ready to tear out the holes
in the body so as to clean the body

we're hungry, we agree on it we are invisid
reachful, arming for the hole in the building

through which we pass, nuggets in our grasp
holding them for food having scraped

of the clearance we give to the child showing him
datives, explorational giving, the little kittens like

fish, we are ready to fish in the thick wet air
we have the little bodies of the eatables

the fine eyes of the

Mid-day

the stream on leaves, giving off ideas without having them through,
she will judge on this one, he disappr

the vengeful aspects are treatable, little round face of the child who
will be

venture, the hammering enclave built in the forest having been
deprived of its central plateau which hovers above in a diving
execution of feeling

proven through the groove times of the plank set, we're for them
afterward telling, in the bottom room of the tor

we're telling them and it sifts up to the top, the tor belt hitting their
motives like the belt flicking cold on hot

the tor belt seat on which the little round child sits ready venturing,
the round wind fat on the hamper through the air that cuts straight
haggles through, his eyes

treat on me, treat on haggle manna straight through the clasp of tor
straight in the hamper we sit inside the

night

the bodies are sleeping, the air sifts through its hasps are rounded car
sweeps, are calm dies flicked through ramparts the coming through
of cluster magnets the bits clump here in tufts the air spreads out the
air wanders in the corner feels the feathery might temperate air
through across your eyelids sleepering brush brush the air brushes
you sleeping the air whirls away again plundered in the middle with
cakes and magnet honey, come cluster here magnet honey, this
thicket's nice with what we'll ever

Sub rosa

In the cleft we hid
forthcoming, the certainty of someone who wants in the door bursting
through with his shoulder the airy certitude the paper he waves in front
of your face the whistle
the comment the arc
placed in front of your
eyes the handle on the door
reaction torso turned your way when you
don't want it the singing
women made out of water the genius for replication the

        line rash element, what
        we had said for us broken
        over our back skin
        seeking the closed eyes
            under the umbrella we can speak
            for that fighting is the same thing as
            the mouth ready to unhand you
        chimes and southerly
        we can handle this, we can order among the asses

The girl hides agile with her
mimicry fragile and eyes
stalled on your heavenly dimensions
What do you do when the door is heaving forward and the

The tromp zone the ice bomb *we see it lobbed*
over our shoulders the ice bomb
lobbed over our chance
participating in the *small slice of crap heaven*
in which they talk defeat

The bin is ready
The bin is ready
We are climbing into it
Idi Amin
Guy Lombardo
singing
near us, singing
with portents
ready to translate us into our own certitude
we got door handles, we got you ideation
by the breadth
eating your crumbles
very sure

Now you tank with substance you
are ready for your nomenclature blues
you are signing us so pretty
flagellant, abrasive, sure of what the back skin

Take it no give it no take it stop you are so cute the way you cut
        the vinyl of your skin is so
        altruistic, made for magical cultures
sure your crap ballistics are made for it
ok *vas y* allocated for it everywhere

ok my nose is running with desire, the cumulative breach
twoness, the line running midbrain
and broken at the same time it sutures, your future
blanked out for it
ready for it in

        noise, the soft beak probing
        noise the talky
        nose the featured
        symbol the break
        we turn from each
        other to turn, we read to each other
speakingly
the soft face scorched to tribe
the soft voice reaching somewhere
it doesn't see
it does

See
you are the wren in the belltower
the soft flesh in the car door
the brain tissue cupping out the bowl of the head on to
street zones, paving them with the measurement we
were looking for we
have found you embarked
a pained expression a cough a hard table called
a desk a warrant waiting a check this
speaking voice a broken
wage earner *all you people come here*
under my wing come here to speak to me
tell your own story of authentic
demolition

                    the side of your body has slipped down and
your loading is taking patience to wait
a fricassee to wait while door and window have no similar patience
getting closer, trailing us
                    your eyes your throat it's getting close
to your aggregate
thigh your trombone stretching out your
stretching out the cha-cha-cha we are in it we

Agree
the best way you are in it you know
damply, configured with the small blood
declining out of you
the transport of admonitory factories
the dishes plastered one after the other
in front of the wall where you stick your
head to breathe and
eat and breathe

The vesper is inside you it
declines your ides of mastery
    it the speaking
    head of the same
portent telling you again
Again the dull yes, the dull no, the building
over there are you here
in the car held again
transfixed by the diatribe, giving it
Up, giving it in

the sky is purple slightly
is a roseate marble stuck deep in your eyes
replacing your ocular throes
You understood what the color said to you
thrust in your eyes about the five minute mark
you amazing marbled toward the wall of the sky
amazing marbled toward the wall
you heard it sound of thumping dull maze meant
The thumping dull sound so sure of itself against
the roseate marble
wall thrown inside
your skin way inside Your torso
is thrown against itself from within
          so prettily effective it
          wants to get to know the face you threw on
the face you made by the roseate hues of the

Inventory, your eyes clicking one by one as the
round scent of the rolling wall goes
          longer, louder, there and there
Chimes, oscillations slow and marbled
eyes peeking up and out, destoried
and ready, the edge of the country looking up slowly
          rolling like a house toward your idea

Misprision

My bracelet privilege is in position since
   not so very long ago a prince, a deluded
truth serum lecturing on a self-destructing
   film theory authored by love, told me

decking and the quibbling arts are nothing
   more than postwar writing pinches.
Recognize the international amnesty for vocabulary
   such as that is counterpart or retrofit

for the animal. I am sixteen I was
   numbered in the project, dorsality thinking back
while thumbing the prosthetic matchbook
   I always keep in my hands, fiddling them projectively

which really means a cart or a horse, he will dress us
   after life on the line pre-jeans, roll on
being the particulates that grant your lunacy
   appeal, discourse of course a book

inanimate on the horizontal surfeit of the desk
   which pitches on the boat you've settled in, the afterlife
of literal Love. A sentimental war
   in apposition to your blood, mana et mana

swells your heart, young of itself and
   rented to come in parts. No no
to the muscle, no no to the bone.

Show me state

your hood under
your letter skin
good now recreate
a beach the bright
umbrellas of cloud
dune ricochet dry
waves smacking down
the sand through you
and that compatriot
photo curtain
donning your robe
and through the stone streets
prohibition wafts the
thin end of your mind

Surprise

a version city knew the same floor
warming a rock sleeper with a shirt
on, sporting an imitative posture
like an artificial film dude
shepherding near his hopes
on a piano, still
we hear in seasonal drapery
wielding a tethered wave
invaded by the designation "red"
and leaping over you in a thin
run, like we're asking you sweet
water well under the trees
near for your letters, a long
smile on the pale truck not alone

Rehearsal

She slept all night
invaded by stars
aversion of events
we like the corner from
the dark transparent
shades the window
dusty with children
tinted in pastel
the silver corner
in the mind's
implied reverse

Bend

Your legs are painful from the fruit your eyes dry from it
so tell me are you rueful as you make out

are you making out with the cold metal
of the girl lying down below the jacket

on the cold sand cold from the night the crabs
come running to the invitation party to the beach

dark invisible from people gone the surface
of the scurrying earth dark with movement

surface parturitioned with merchandise
people smiling with teeth bare and blazing

the malnutrition of the beach bare with blazing
the sun blazed out with a person waiting, waiting

for you to be done you're done you've
finished fished you have scraped it all
out of you at last you are fishless you are finished

the sand bare of crabs
the street bare of cars or legs

the walking brain inserted back into the head
you are bent from the stick you are bent from

the canister you are inserted into the canister
of your bent legs back again into the intended

stream against which your legs rolled, waves
of comprehension tensile in your flat decanted

in the breakers of your limbs and back
again your eyes promising outward to

a someone blank complaining of your hours
you're allotted you're a lot to take in
you are a lot on the ground of the earth a plot

inside your ear an assemblage constant to yourself
a little story to tell a story to keep you fed

in your mind inside there totally silent in there
telling yourself the blanket or the cave, the spread-out

story of the anthropods who're doing it, sane as mice
sane as hospitals, the arms stretching slowly out
to grace you with the Plans of Gently Doing It

the slow settling of the barter, the exchange
we give each other eating with our eyeball teeth

come smiling to stop what you are doing
now from want to make a worker in the world

you take and give and breathe and in collapsing
on the grass at last you bend

National Anthem

In the inland   mouth
from the leave   sore
bending   in the stomach
sore from statehood   in your
knees where   they cleft in
your vagina or   your in-head
legs the ears   sore from
dogs barking   flat from
scratch to rip   we're sore from
listening to risk   the plangent
animus of will   or whether it'll be
a that or be   remember or a
problem figurine   it's either way
you covey it   your britches
overspread   with ladled shank or
edges pushing out   the more
you thank   your welcome

Present tense

Minute 1: sure of the import and
its sudden shut brain hazard
need bipartisan. sure and the window is
bright and heavy, we are stone thermometers
torso wedged.
    Minute 2: looking and haphazard
has achieved itself the shoulders of another
limbs are looking at the end of your fingertips
a perfect instance being
      Minute 3: others
must be somewhere silent on the phone
only a slice of the corporeal
earth will be arranged collapse might
anyone needs to hear. Minute 4: what
about that airwaves, no blue ink in
dynamo curves. a corrective
mis-states the case, takes it somewhere else.
you kept the adamant constitution where?

It makes inside the one world.
      Minute 5:
with freaked ideas perfectly
aligned with what it's possible within
by muscular intrusion. So he says. The one
without as popular editions let us down
as referees, commandoes, love interests
couldn't even break away from understanding
half together. It would have been a pamphlet
to have seen.
    Minute 6: Buddhists give great site
great attitude yielding pleasant to
compliant, but I already have a job.
That area to each other's stony yielding

to the table, poking your hands out to eat
and show your food.
                              Minute 7: there

was a moment of breath, the blue ink

waves coming out of hand, slowly

assembling the listeners then out the door

Minute 8: I have put an ocean between me
which turns around the earth and doesn't fall
off hearing there innumerable wires
chest to wave. I assume the music goes
one way, the person doesn't choose.

The law's a soft machine fondling your forehead

her hand trembling in the known
She was in the kitchen in the lounge in
the tree barking she was barking in the
tree and we knew we were vincible
in knowing the real in rendering
her a barking of the hot soft
real breaking on the machinery of
the chair and tabled, the plastic of
the eye on you sabled rendered
real by Plastic wish the mind as tune

on instrument on her hand the real time
telling the soft muscles tensed for giving
the animal eating the plastic offspring the
machinery of the real giving way
at last a plastic time Enormity giving
way (and holding) and holding

up a barking from the tree a made up
stroke a mind bent outward to the plastic
bark so they can hear the dog across the valley
stream machine real giving place
like we administer the plastic aliments
really upon her skin she spoke the altruistic
(posed upon her skin) she stretched
her mind she treed us out she gave it

out her legs bent screeching she was bent
back in the plastic story and could not

believe her self that story real
besot Supposing the allotted
river boat the elegant woman

finally giving to soft floating
on the mind the plastic eyes resolve
with looking glasses On her ears
the soft machine of the mind blent
plastic tendrils reckoning out disharmony
the real fins sharping her translucent
skin her Barking in the tree
they have her in have made

a very fine one indeed the others
hanging at tree ends soft the tree
beautifully they time a talk they angle
their bent legs underneath a wrecked
(compact entailment) with complete smiles
the machinery of the real She's given to the
smiling gun of the real the bag
on the table perched glass
bodies on trees the instrumentalizing
know They perch there barking
in the real the long-head figurines
this long are holding any glass (they hold her
bodies) happy to be further stretches where
were echo for the barking glad

shadows on the table near her head where holding
graciously her Nearby telling
archer (budding tree)
to grow the scrotum of a real compose
yourself museum, building, make, your poster of
the real, inset The tree case of the humming
warm (on case) the soft bake harbor pressed
against her side Her arch amiss
the tree a disappearing complement of

speaking without vocals score or implement
the glass is dead nor disemboweled
plastic tree beside you me
the soft flat of the tree amiss you
my the top arch boat on which
you gesture hard perfume
between we may

Modern Love

The mirror's back a door her
allegorical and struck propriety knew
she would breathe the possible
freight from each assembly
why the social was another tongue
he hadn't reproduced the neighborhood
she was seeing whips on out the back
a series of ultra flagellants
whose ropes erase as well another
image set extension cords
across the interstate she
flinches from the feeling *floating*
letters go above their bled compartments
tentacles were kept for us hand-held
and sewn in back I cannot
make my torso keep my head

Press the image

Of echo tacitly inclined
Of outset raintree we
The wiry bounding line remained
So kiss, so roundtree flatten out
Yourself a kine of earthly substantives
Amiss apart from concrete blocks
You're wearing on your head
Avoid me now
Simmer on the premise multiple
Slams of industry coming for you
Waiting in the sardors
Flat inside shadow we press
Ourselves nomenclature durable
Ourselves a premise opened for
A moment of incline upon
Which we slope

Defensively, the elevator
Doors coming apart to cleanse
Us now, the selfsame pickets
We hold our eyes to keep them open
Fairytime at the last, the singular
Admission holding the doors open
For perdurable ingress
Has besotted you imposture
Drift, the flake of admonition
Which you wash with a smile scraped
Across your cheek a speaking
Wince, a fine agon of airy
Multiplicity astew, your facile
Nondeterminants sprecking
For a breath, holding the invisible door
Open a moment, longer

Breed

Pendant notorious rhetoric capable of
nothing   commissioned by dumb show
trumpt ample
speaking silence in the dominant
                truggling

eloquent subtlety indoors
   already in a torrential self-sensitive
    city overwhelmed
   by reduction!
             holding him by the hand
           a posthumous suasion

   in silence hugely the rafter   ambience at the

first sight of equivalence

Don't talk to me

Silence is a self-conscious acoustic
explosion against the pitch

                    you sweet
       the air allay   ethereal waters
the ordering charms of art have gabbled you

You turn in the skin

   Sound is a crux in your absent mouth
hyperbe unspeaking   a peculiar
        torn of utterance

  smoked into the floor implicitly
                   if you
                command
  take no direction use your common

        still as possible – folio
   considerable disement think

            histrionic, improply
  on the stage you are totally

Acting after

submitting
long pause long silent gaps   deliberate bale

arrested within hearing
compounded silence takes the stress of
all speech whilst
our dialog is prejudiced with significance

At the window, every shirt

Signal failure listening to meals
whoosh by the treatment of freedom

perceived as

one who is walking in air

perceives
unless the movement of the head is marked by
moral force. Capacity for silence performed

draw to me.

Moreover precisely. Delineate
the orchestra opened its mouth

She moves over to where

to speak, restricted to silence
      either metrically   or your hands   on the bows

we fell. The pliant use trice drawn along the courtier's
                              vanquished air.

A distress froze
stopped through
the lines like episodes!

Performative custody

     consuming   candor   vivid
         of the silence   in place of nature
we get
close
and closer to the master island silenced
                        the bull is silent

     the pronouncement   speaks   us silly
   rapture   in the speak   now silent

these quiet calculations with
arise the quick complication of imagined textual failure

Glue

what looks like you might actually be amphibious
an opium syllable
every deploy has actually been made

      a famous stage mark bracket two start lines

like a   *come thou ratify my gift*
how talk they
     in the briney sussuration of style she finds
     sufficiently common veer

expressive force of suppertime
the arms and legs have work to do
they prop up premises
who's talking   enjoining one's newer present
                      daughter mother
              chased me quickly through
         the wet anxiety near the salt it isn't
always night

Reenactment

a pale man with a pause came in the water
two briars bright remorse expectant *pause*

we are fleshed in the flesh of the water
never unalloyed neither separate or expect

near want of gentleness I weaned a weird
retreat stoke rather in the *pause*

a peril's kiss and minimal exchanged
rich silt of ribald exultation stood the text

Detourment

in the oracle then a glass orb floated
down she swallowed it broke
inside her restoration birth of the
broken she felt at the rupture moved
her lower half near back part

tail flowing end split force art water
impossible to see the mute embrace as though
the glass air were
include her breathable

                                      sweet now our marred start
                           sembling you the landscape this enormously

Promissory

we see the blood is coursing
perturbed *of course* it's
upset it wants the images of
want with the full-length sky
images, the flat isotopes of
earth you can see it here
clearly in the project on the ceiling
so *you do not have to sit up* look
it's here the area of darkness is
cognizant telling you its uptake
cognoscenti in the black and
white is fuzzy here the scan
in which the color sites resolve
on which one sees oneself unable on
the quid pro quo of tacit levitation
by way of covenant convincing you
we wire shut your mouth until
such time as *safe to open it*

Unfamiliar dog

wrestling on the mat
dialog in hand, he barks
the manual waiting to hear
he barks and the mat
lists

liaison perking up in mask she
perks up to the ask
and tells the chain heft
drawn and louche
her ply a square floor
plough is stuff enough

for books and plea
a wonky managed filler
for the set blast take
off something huffing just
for you if life is
crew enough

if bark, the pat soft
placate deck
waiting for whose dialog
with figures
stick

Thirstory

Brilliant country, butte of the children
spit anointed everything

towing his main terms, who first did

after rain and excellent
                    nth mediate body
in other respects carried
        bridges and condition

nor of range, the sin of personal promise
moved by lot
in proof he summed on
free posts
very like to dress, to this, to drink on his clothes
                        and was mistaken
        guise arc in

being so great he played   the cove he hid in
                over to her, fused on my heap, on occasion
            offering and the birth
without a head by

                                portent

    by the wise mean eaves
            dreamed a still
        more piece of pliant

Oh no don't sweep it I
am dense with it, named
you were spherical or was
your conical ambivalence part
of what held the door
immensely open all that while after

after all who kept the keys
asleep up finding no ready
hand secretly moved
a hair of gold and
fend us manfully

by him crossing on return
   successive
   it, slack and next to

near the body, not upon
the face, picked up

up by the lax tongue

   where it hit him in
   the forehead

where he differs most

   from seeking, from soft

   falsehood in an inventor of
round witness of scribes and that
   the case ire dominant by

that cleft

arms

He disagrees the time
was not fled from him
to be loaded
                              and afterwards
              war hout taining a   decisive or but learnt

     dropt ather, and if voluntarily
                         made men and women ad feat
        a large taken brother and leased
                              ex arch

a city of advice set wooden walls
taken by a vision

Since death lies caustic
                  fuge to the chains, and loosed hir heads
        on spire to release   him under

cure, under lightning   flash flesh, brilliant

throwers and archers, fetching   completely
                         to see

        unguarded   until suddenly
              in ambush and flight
under the thigh

                                    after
        the sun had destroyed itself we stood there

                sideways, the result of a cunning
                compress of multiple points

        on the brink, clunky with haste
        suaded by sooth and scent
                        being the ropes
                                strong talisman, strong
                words he licked them and

two-beaked words we would
hand back and forth

we dangled on for years, feeling

Ship

You go to sea your chest is tight
a band of wire inside
it's like that when the man you were
to paint you let and language
high like Moby Dick, the bending of the wood
over its principal arc. Other women too
and you are not a sign of broken finitude
when Someone shows up at the door
whose apricot provisions field
will stand and heal or stony nests
were sometimes on the floor
his iron sites the vacuum pump.

Nearby the window stirs
in disarray you are not born
back into death your feet are inward shod
your tongue gets clear to writhe again
the wet spools complement you on
the velvet fabric backs against
your side. The heavy suitcase holds its full
impatience with the bridges fall and tip
laughing with the social world the rooms
inside the telling theorist vomited a
streamlined utterance of the deck
you walk your little dog with no causation
forward back nor formal someone says
and what is that

Mariner

I rem
up in dis
stance cushion
mirror drag
float on
your spe
cifically flax
bound roam

field your
rotund gave
one more
leg pair

us both
dogged
with wet

I rem
on the gold
hill dog set
walk to the
building's other
side, sweet dog

Beaming cry

I'm just trucking the backward
liking careful the plastic
riff back up my skin I let it

greater than a better now it
goes where you know it lighter
than a shuffle of the tempered

feet arrive and play
the pools your eyes
they played a light sword

starting out with thunder
thru the premise of acculturation
blinds a retrogression of

the thumb you press
your teeth you keep
your promise eyes

Postcolonial postcards

1

The car is blue this time and howling
pedagogue: what's missing is an obvious
pain of view. If you "put yourself out there"—
that is, dissimulate, a given we call to rather
elder pillars set self-love
at the terminal we're stopped.

2

A function of encounter inheres in your
tautology until I grab your hand:
Analysis: why bother anyway?
Telling is an amateur device reserved for
substances: acetate, the immolation of desire
There she said "discipline" (discipline)
Well yeah I think so
capsized without fear.

3

The half-edged cry of gulls the screech
of cars like whales very sorry indeed
who've sacked themselves
with grief lures secrecy impatience
makes a point that doesn't hurt
beyond the novel we rather enjoyed.

4

He had been ruined
Publicly made
ruination his heritage

storytelling catachresis at a standstill
Which of us is not
whole? I might mention
the watch, the eyes
rolling along the wall.

Narrative poem

In the planks are tread
on the wheel by virtue of
the house. You have no blight nor
camera for a chamber
the wheels on the house are turning the wheels
on the eyes of the planks
underneath your feet. You walk like a camera
toward the tree you glow

amidst a sound charades
the shaft of glowing wall
cleft in repair on which a man rests
his back warm on the stone. He is the warm stone
healed, a rattlesnake perched
round his boot crushed gently
under the gun, smoothly quietly
the rattlesnake under his warm stone.
In the gentle forenoon the arrows
on his back décor an afterthought

soft parameters rejoined—the tree is tall and thin—in the yard devoid
of enginery—the man with the warm fan spreading out—through the
vegetables a theory of awake.

*

The suitcase flapped in the living
room décor seepage, some fluid from between
the little mammal glowed safe
keeping—a small aperture open in the box pebbles falling out—one by
one the engine room
mouth keeping. Hours in
the character, the yard honed
smooth in a rail machine

that's fine, a warm command
of music up and down surrounded
with a sound of eyes all over the paper
making it, the clenched spine cuckoo
like the yard bird pluming the tree on which you sit
through a yard speaking, the bird
speaks in the box squared out and
worshipped box we seal

your boney hands are flicking—flicking on the case—caparison of skin
against the sheet of glass—pressed on the paper glass—all day
making the day, perched in the glass.

*

The house at the hill is on the paper without
sound, its image convenable
while you make out the other
watching side reparably
making a case, a collection of grasses for the mammals
to win on the room stretched back
like the footsteps overhead, safe
not coming. The movement
of the building toward you avalanche slow drift, the
walking to you fail safe
room in sitting through
the avalanche packed out of
doors you there.

*

A bird is throwing at the wall
glows at the sky of the tree now
a board across your mind which is
the sky throws itself at the bird
thrown through a forest where a fence appears
flash distinct from a bird flash through
sky in the fence at your mind.

*

Edged at the middle
wizard on the fan
walking the fan edge
held for waft machine.

On our weights
on the soft edge
grasses, the apologia
of the green you
stand, grooming for
bodies toughened
up in shift the move
the turning liquid
from the whizzed ides
to the square green now

newness opening—with bloated looking up the face a liquid
image self exuding to participate—pretty for groan pretty for slide—the
screens around their shuck and caw you miniaturize tangle—made
for it the water tower form you—miss like fire spread on your arms—
conventional newness having you again your head ringing with—fondle
your sides as holding quietly on context

*

we're in waking on the square, the dove
levy hefted near the engine room gone
for silent shuffle, the trees might avenues
power totally inside. The water's square
invention paid a tier, a canopy
who ate them with thick smile, the face
pressed through the wood now
with a came, the arms hello.

Drink me

in the small right back small of it
   ah in the weight has sentences
tell me
      thy glorious   lip
                  on summons
      you to an order
            cooling your hands on
water can press
         the button   where
         distribution gets arranged
            and see the small hands
wrapt around the non-
enlightenment we use
when we compose
         the small of your face upturned
to me here with material ah. sentences.

Right to be

Having emulation as your fervent
gaol, having the tongue turned
                        back toward the brain
                    el abuelo materno
where is that
place up
under dermis
                seizure
                    cacerolazos in a moment
                entra con manto de cinezas
                    el propio templo
                    del destructivo *relaxed*
    in the arms or nest
      constituent to actually
    ingress spoken
        to each other each flat
      gesture synched
                e.g. you speak
          the compass answers
back what language
                folds your brain far in
                back what language
wet electric
battery-powered eyes
plugged on your human
            head
          stance trusion
          you know that and
walking on the street
                somewhere you have or no
Right to be
spreak or pandemonium
on the news from

              sprech nor
            sprain you read
the western claims
            along that street
         shield
                    people's ghosts nervy
         girls with voices
         the boys with vocal en
               la palma de sus manos
held in spare keep
resucitar chingolo
      para la culpa
         innombrado in your
                     brave calculave
en una nube se asoma
               I can hear you in a see
               saw pattern
               in your search
for pressings image in
delirium   con rocio
            when you "go external"
and the tissues
take in atavistic
   names you didn't plan
      comprension join
                  your flesh starts
   por los propios
   monjes
                  I can hear you
through the dense glas of your skin
      yo simplimente decirlo

Listen Honey

Trumped with a glass non
-aleatory tired limbs holding
clumped shoulders closed
the road meanders
not at all

Not at all crimped
in your pasture with the girls
and limbs holding
          not at all

He fiddles with the radio and gets
comforts the hearing
all the hills leaning
forward in his eyes
not at all

The "land of freedom"

for Marguerite Porete

I studied in the wastes of Carolina that year little nunnies
reading to each other gently burying blossoms in end words
purple and his girl, like that trope of set 'em up, I talked

refurbishing sacked heroics cunning primitives on form,
working hard on trilogies whose microcosms are syllogistic
they're on language, trying to be both memorable and
forgetting people to have heard, that night and that system
rank their heaven having left behind a lovely blue circle

in the middle where he was to have read his own neoclassical
honeymoon, coming home from a v-shaped subway
of *relief* with all these people at night on the curve, her heart filled
with happy and laughing on the doorknob the gentle skin

so small of a picture certainly not of this street or pavement
skin cadenza, numbers like good schooling keeps you habited
with the coming-to, penumbral exhibitionists maybe
like coming on her face the tears in the difficulty, a kind of
sounds-more-like more-situational kind-of *he said*

he was re-striped, site walls propping the young ideas
as still developing wet photo strips dangling by chance
in April, a student of jet-set words on broad high useful
struts, *all I remember is love*, staring blindly at the quickness
of pulling the catacomb along behind you, the full declaration

of the night filled with sitting alone on the curb, a small
picture in its hands and the picture is of course night taught
in a counsel never to be sorry, hours pressed like leaves in its own
outline tuning or otherwise leaving comments that need
to be depreciated, *I mean that's why the lights are out that's why*

it's night, betweenhand they have options, some of the street
laundries, some lannets slanted on plan, some of the hands
went up for alternatives that were presupposed open, text
on the body of sound from one bluff to another, collaborating with
odds more paint than print, spoken seriously for serial

reasons, feel these small bumps of ideas pushing slightly
out on flowers out of strong frets rising from lineal
absorption one recalls not just images but a nonce field, a division
of the truce we set ourselves our lives out there or inhering literal
infixing of harmonic peculiarities, their views

cribbed out huge ways, color-coded flight patterns across the
window dance of limbs and torsos, running abysmal, filling in
funeral boxes, filling in flower boxes, filling in the sac of your
mutineer *done gone to have wont* a turn about the garden fleeced
by books all muddled up for intimacy themes, like critical
incontinence I wanted to make an argument by doing

closer, the absence of a disquieting manifestation invaliding
Herrick in his summons, they're coming through the flowers
in combinations of stunt, beryl a lovely stint a memory of digging in
her skin in the incident of sexual experiment, living the text and

wedging a whiff on flowers, finally having her darling breeze
gabbing with rosebuds, flicked on time's thug skirt he picked a
shell and biologically motivated the sugar, white on crystal blown

through steam, down to ministerial hands in the garden cool
melons soft boxing the moon on a blue eyewitness, scaled
every day and climbed through for night's minor strings
listening to cheery faces totally misaligned with tilted

men, men on bridges, men on obtuse triangles, participants acute
for ring doffs, has this one come along does she really have
a lightly pelted clue, is there *is there a shoulder lean to*
making pestled process boxes white, the world handing them

boxes of material to sift through with images that connect
with love, images that don't connect with missing time I could
go back but look the crystalline tree anyway knew *I needed
a pale text, I was really looking for that*, my very own

tiny rose on knees and pushed on lumps, an open-ended
chaos orchestra set in thirty movements next in line
huff and a high ceiling sound "the" as in "feh" or
"Christ" aperture on said vocal drinking here

said coming thru felt in thickened heal and sure
your derrick habit odd on said, your system pages formed by
shocking, shocking under a morsel dirt on light you made
what you said clear on report nor clearly cold, the wind
chill lined straight front, inveigling into the outlines

you open the fruit trees and there obtain notes
ripening in the tiny rips, calm for small arrivals lit from your
programming's full weight, even the pirate's force is facial, the
eyes in large part yield those heard, canticles fade on wield

they believe in modern pleasure all over, long the wrist-held side
of urban heat you scotch through bones in your skin whose
hidden cover turns out to be a warm wet sheet you can pull from
in your skin like that, pulling hard and almost Andalusian not

uncomfortable anyway, healing normative water, air on here her
face as collision, a haunted wind on healing and a strategist
meaning that pushes on calm ahhh, resident in the word sound
music felt initial here a density of noise in broad strokes

treat on flow, the garden road and its tangible stroke lights
what delirious nausea or what Texas seeing, clocks washed
over with water and mood, your eyes jetting to the rain as though
gelatinous marble quell, storm on stroke and borders *but what is
actually said*, the walls over index scattered by a face

light sympathy with terminal wooing screen, with scold water
and balloon figures baby-ridden status consequence they're
here and here, coddled lapse and fumble walk with her
by the established field strumming the shore graph pitch

dark thump, *I am born again* in a blue stroke, green ditch
shaft and an image that could be nothing but sound-lacquered
shoulder gaps, a cover like someone walking beside you
hangs much like tiered graphics at the waiting table

rainbow circumscribed over their plates, foursquare woven
cup, tangled water rushing toward it her hand crave on
gentle carcass wafted by with said big bundles, huge bundles,
scored on sound strokes windless, she turned toward how

you came to be lying there like the observational body
and the lips, a jumble really *shhh* triptych mirror birth port
thwap and grill fled sound shriek compress on the marble of
your listening head, whirr whirr glint on said, glint wrecked

the tangle wrecked a heretofore winced ancestor: they seem
welded, interest look on scale, collage scored deep a gentle
negativity or whatever with assumption boxing through
a wood uncertain of capital, they hang about the extant score
having written together we read together at tables

chairs, clothes, long streamers of paper hands set overhead, what
do they mean lying amongst sculpted wooden flutes, doom said
why not knit that in despite, not to our kin but our disposal
infinite cavities in verse through which your fingers fall in form
and cover ask or missing industrial women self-committed

hey destiny, whose area makes a Euro-avant longitude, let me
quote on the end of my lord the swan, tilt on its tail hairs light as
fair as general felt in hand, existent or a void writing into past
possible, after math has taught you to add you to yourself do then

accumulate liquid difference between receptivity and a song
for facsimile chanting, string instrument adjectives furious and
decidedly long, a high laugh making historical sound outdoors
whilst inside minion chore materials love them, such as

object and process, or queer destiny hyping trace contours
page shape limited, assessment as a spiritual ease wired across
a pen or around on will firm in the mind, its narrative arc
disrupted by breeze about a world in cleft, found or not

found together, disclosure: they're not down on youth cares
shellacking bandwidth drives toward sacerdotal burning,
why just this morning access to a pattern more or less doing
the whale upturned a gentle drawl, donated a future no longer
sure of ten-part sequence turns, remodeled Orpheus again

Singularity

The wind not stet the harpers holding out. The wind
not stet the harpers holding, the woman in the house
holding branches then trees not stet on holding out out.

The holding hands with the new the girl on the hillside up.

The meaning fabric tear it out the tears gone finical the
high waste machinery the mechanism the tear the holding
hands the mud mud. The bed the holding frame
the holding there up up tear the holding hands
the people holding breath the breath coming up
up the lungs holding the lungs held
the hands holding stare back waste machinery
the pumping bright holding hands stare machinery
the hallway the light clothes of the holders the hands
waster machinery the bachelor holding hands
with the held the eyes bright on soft closed inner the beatitude
the beat beat

crimp the hand holding softer the frame the bed
the eyes holding hands with halls white clarity
as structure wherein holding hands surcease.

Out in the blue may heft out in the may.

Heft it out in the holding hands may when the held
eyes in the cup of the holding tear hands the brown house
the white house the blue house the red house the green

house the sky the aft husbandry the walking
down the sidewalk followed by someone who is not
you not never will be, sideways rift
monitor moved to the hall, sidebar grafted ceremonial,
the movement of the arms into clothes, the feet
into the dormant flat ground underneath the total wedge
heft particle the moment you

Face down (triptych)

a wave-like animal when you tur
                    n it
        follows you in t
    o the sluicing
            pearls of your tor
so'd brain the same fre
                    quence
            thee of
    motion is
        a tourni
quet for motored acci
            dent equations on

The autoliner speaks
the boat hums and roars
guggily, a bandwagon
        we're all on ex-officio, a da
                fit rancor of a
    momentous
            give   n to steam en
            gines
                gas engines, the heart and ears
                    roaring their approval
falling man reprobate on the hinge
the bridge a flash toward auto

liner measurements the h
              and upon
the tankard car like
         stance you re
    mind yourself is ease or
    vacan
         cy, the stubble on
    this   haven skin you
mind yourself one black
  and white black bird flung
              to
         ward
         the waters of the sky
    your list on
  hinge done that
bright yellow float
bestirred on instrument

Day

My broken chest whose pottery is nomenclature gone solid.
I was going to I was going to in the breach there is a provision only this
or I could stand and talk to you directly.

I have swallowed a large stone the carcass of possibilities.
It gets heavier and heavier like writing.

In the morning she distributed a fragment, glow in the forehead
between the eyes. The cannibalistic shut-fence between embodiment
and languor.

Minutes later, I am flushed hot, then cold as stone. Holding
hands in the dark. At night the heat flicks on and off, the keys strophic,
blood like a pan heating the clump inside the torso pulsed with ringing,
stomach, held muscles, holding my head against her forehead, the life
from one to the other, his smile at the chocolate, the gene sequence
dialing out and out the genes in disarray you are supposed to take
everything with equanimity, everything.

The blue blouse light and racking, fattening up in the light room high
in the ship of the house, *meaning to meaning to I was going to*

Cones

See with cones, the yellow axiomatic thru your pillars

see with strait refines, the kids kick flat to

dice, see the rectangular fibrillation

tropospheric, your lips drawn tight around

tremulous excuse the wet filtration system

your eyes enlarged to get around

see, the eye opened and stretched all round

the object inserted to the eye to see

the thrilling invitation in your mouth

stretched wet around exception

see the tongue pushed back the vision

large inside your eye's inversion splayed

across the rectangular field, see

it's pushed see it accepting all the way

Haptic radio

Sitting across in April without intent
to draw warm on your own hands
blow
where I textually imagine you
entirely of paper wet from the boat

I rev in distant cushion
stance on the radio chair
mirror drag flat
on your specially flax-bound roam

you look one more pair of legs been
making us technological labor

Take the limit case over to the sofa
against a wall where birds are centrally
repeated on the pulse

        where are you from?

      imaginative work maintains the social world
      impaled on blue skies
          drenched with sugar paint
    above the patent grass delivery by
                a sign whose irate
            running in the car
      the baggage by the birds next to the telegram

playing in your inner eye
inflated to the size of an insurgent
were not smelted with solemnity, not

birthday cake on the dripping
paints *aroha* dismantled straight

(tap tap) - - - - - - -

We were visible on the wire
my fingers executed through tone
for example the tiny floater
rubbed by a stranger
mistaking my face for his own

on the chair not answering
or a cluster
        good we had and a tall cloth forest
against the sky projected by our all-seeing
eyes on the furniture

        your ease to please shine
where
        you're gifting your eidetic principles
        say it with me

turning on the table
with dystopic birds
tanked by fashion, by the bestiary
years after the event of her landing

from the air straight to the target
of her dreams

- - (tap tap) - - - - - -

    Everyone is totaled where your rites

           come close, and closer to my own judicious

    compliance, faltering with ease I am finally
    talking with my ears and you are
         listening with your mouth

the only visitor, burnt wood in a composition
my guide had intensified
the bridge like a foremast on our shoulders

We planked pacific basin
placated the obedient reproach
        each minute now I'm various
as though we stand outside
logs at our feet
a clamorous temerity in concrete circumstance
the extra merchandise our limbs almost
vicarious, our strategy breeds
society as itinerant combination

drake of the waves
homestead has collected the birds and hangs
in the corridors overhead

As a result, knife till
basin mortifies the water
to find the peeled-in skin

they stood as bodies without falling
though their nerves were far apart as
from the sky were held return

- - - - (tap tap tap) - - - - - - - - - - - - -

Listen to the strings
listen to the tin theatre
your belly between one house and another
two months and you'll be strong dominant
speaking by the rift of a sea where stung by salt
floated in the grass you constant
daystream wanting, holding your lips and be
magnanimous to a partial serenade

To be happy we walk on
the names of the softly buried

I approximately I stand and weep in the known

ground someone surfaced wet and cast

soft bells, a story of earth forms
run along the water
          planks, a cool bench tin water
comfort at our stripes by the parade

That happened a year ago we give comfort to
balloons, configuring topsides
a palate tucking ambient polemics
          this day of attention more
          sublimate than actually told

          - - - - (tap) - - -

The building is partial innocence
you always say grey harbor touching strokes

          we stick a needle in the custom house wall
          and wiggle it until history comes out

applauded for adrenal whims
the crying of a portion dreams thereafter

The industrial revolution was succeeded by
a technological no, infinity is a number
I have come to understand immensely
       stout
          and variable in the hands
          we're holding
marginalia at a pass from one
landing to the other
part your legs don't usually
          touch natural accretions of a text
          where one sits
theoretically at a table
          that is always at the half-way point
          of a peripheral mind, a real time book

          you read it closed
          nearby the fetish page
          exotica of the lisp

familiar flattened publicans as
surrounded with explanation, heavened to death
by intrigue where we're eating
in the basement listing everything

The man with the spoon

Approaches simply. it is the dance of the thousand veils. the man on the boat watches the profile, if she moves he will. they cry together without the other being aware. the man with hands swings across buildings, car to car. very fine weather adores him.

Neoclassical jealousy has formed the seats from an ambient material overlain with plasticine making a position for how we love each thing. it has become impossible to construe a life without value. speak to the approaching man with sympathy or integrity. the book finished itself, fluttering shut its pages in a substitute

overheated mouths approaching depth without a paradigm to wield them. to speak without value, the man makes an analogy of the coat hanger touching our skin with a coral reef very far away. the ambient technologies of the reef are planting a salt sword face up in the approaching subject.

Aristotle's pen

Clear amber feathery filigree explains
its nylon paths were never more interesting
as slapping your own hand across your face

beside the fit of arteries
a copper-hour fallen
on the hubris of my back

Etched little whirligigs
like the answer to the boy across the street
"Don't wait for me!"

As though the eyes peer forward to see light
themselves create ahead a flashlight
world imagine it

as limbs to manifests stuck out
to circumvent the circle that's erased
with glossy wiring, holding it in place.

Political flesh

We have an in with savvy
particles
hitting ornaments while the castle
winks
auspiciously devout, tweaking the
quick-thought agreement we made
wherein
sweet odors settle milkily around
the assembled cups tall hope lying

or a tune will, skin like paint like dust and
file to set you breathless, the tight
will
of the girl giant hovering over the odors
building a micro-set of virtues
with
paints like setting in the dark
nor sky nor dog nearby but dictates

in an enraptured future tense
we'll climb a ladder made of knives
whose
all extremes hold fervent to
a test of sorts, a witness
woman
looking at the ghost of her own
forehead quick with latitude

avenues grow
dense and winds
come quickly keeping
the stone warm
with persistent breath
whose exhalations
garnered and outré
as a girl's hands
lightly sew a
thread of veins
into the counterpane
of a grass bed
knowledge of itself
congruous lends
protection to the visible
from arrest
becoming glad
becoming nailworn
numbers blankless
self-looped idol
dark held soft
a swell whose
counterpanes lift
cometed
dissever

Peephole metaphysics

Listening for you listening notes for right to seek up

futures as a buffer against permanence can you make

actuality not a matter of argument I'm sirry I'm political

ready to drag down changeable as the crew people

jumping in to small boats showing their interest

without necessary attributes to be hot, so hot

sirrah listening to the heart boats bombing are you

new to the names amidst your hectares get along

new to your improves on several hats beside the year's

tasted aperture months ready to open pour in

astonished to discover mouths underneath the boats

craggy as fashionable creamy broody belts in range

out of range the edges of the heart mouths totally

unsteady drama groovy coming along worth trying

to sell our inherited personalities for settlement when

people came here they planted themselves in utterly familiar

and hills coming along at the edges of the heart

mouths planting the recognizable in water at the moment

falling through the atlas trope sway comprehensive

for another album of highlights everybody getting a little

somefin a tiny mouthful louche over the skin of the teeth

a point especially clear when terms of value broken

across the example becomes clear a like simple

economy of scale transient as the top blend came on

a simple feat hot off the head as hundreds rippled

like scales real as existence marbles tottling on

the edges of the site kept at it fully every rim

consistent turning square to diamante pusher

folly coming along saying flask as catskin blueberry

rich or cast is it what you expectation frag there

slightly animistic with an absolute forearm

or what it means to compromise with cultural life

as you make room make room stead skulldigger

in a roaring mind the trophy on your head your own

juggy code out at the stuck late skin in show

I often kilter or a separately repeated to see how

it changes a man with a fixed expression in plastics

a cast as what you expectation frag there yes

Love

The pinks of the dead are fly by night bees
holding your hand as you fly next to me
your underwear tangled with clouds
singing to your flesh with a front
fixated tremor with your holding hand
stains on your lips course lollipops
near your episodic nature of love
alongside sycamores whoosh recurrent
having held your content do I find
projected via wheel rights nearly
sodden through panting in
the original ion I do know
whole places most of your limbs
fly off aesthetically diverse
texts kind of glance
squirming near sidereal
give a copy of their topics
imminent so I half wish
I were sugar curled
girl across last ifs